What Exactly Are You Thinking?

Original artwork copyright Ben Crane,
from a caricature sitting.
Used by permission.

What Exactly Are You Thinking?   2

What Exactly Are You Thinking?

By
Pammy Jo

A Politically Incorrect Guide to Living In Harmony with the Opposite Sex . . . .

WHAT EXACTLY ARE YOU THINKING?

To contact the author or to order additional copies of this book:

Pamela Allemand Hubbard
PO 647
Big Horn, WY 82833
307-673-1417

- - - - - - NOTE TO READERS - - - - - - -

A SINCERE THANKS

I would like to thank all of my friends, family and acquaintances for sharing your opinions, situations, screaming, crying, drinking, throwing things, it has all helped me to write this book. I would also like to thank the ones of you who have had to listen to me rant & rave about my own situations! I've certainly had my share over the years!

You may see yourself a few times in this book, but just know you aren't the first or last to be in that situation. Hope you like it, and certainly don't take any of it personally!!!

Second thought-- if the shoe fits, go ahead and slide your foot into it!!
Happy reading . . . .

What Exactly Are You Thinking? 6

CONTENTS

What Exactly Are You Thinking? 8

FOREWORD -

First of all, I would like to say that I am not a doctor or therapist. I am just an average, maybe a touch over-achiever, middle-aged, married woman trying to figure out why it is so difficult for a man and woman to live happily ever after in this world. It seems no matter who you talk to, it is the same saga, the women blame the men and the men blame the women. There are some couples that will actually tell you, they couldn't be happier, I personally think that is total bullshit, but then again, maybe they have it all figured out and should be the ones writing this book!

There are a couple statements that seem to have stuck with me, "Happiness is not that life is perfect, it is what you make of it" (You need to live life to the fullest each & every day) and "Don't sweat the small stuff." (Most things in life are small stuff) If you are goofy enough to think you can be happy 100% of the time, you need to snap into reality..., ain't gonna happen!

This is just my opinion, of course. In fact, this whole book is just my opinion, so you are all welcome to agree or disagree.

I am not saying this book will solve any, or all of your problems. In fact, it may cause a few, if neither of you are willing to do a little changing or just can't handle hearing the truth about yourself! At the very least, I hope a few people will take the time to read it, stop and think about a few things, and try to do something to make life a little happier. Life is too short to be unhappy.

This book is written about what I consider is the "general" population; I realize there are exceptions to all of this.

Though, sometimes it's not all bad to be the exception...............

Chapter 1

ARE WE REALLY THAT DIFFERENT?

We all know there are some differences between women and men; this is not a news flash!! It has been this way since the beginning of time. I just get tired of everyone putting the man up on a pedestal and having it left up to the woman to treat him as he prefers to be treated, not a lot is mentioned that the man should show equal respect towards the woman. That he ought to treat her as he would want to be treated.

I realize back in the day, things were a lot different, but let's face it; we no longer live, "Back in the Day". I think both men and women want, and need a lot of the same things out *of life: to be <u>respected,</u> loved, admired, and trusted. I think if you truly respect someone, the rest of the wants and needs will follow.*

A lot of men want to live like we are still in the 1930's. They don't want to change at all. A lot of them still think there is a difference between "men's work" and "women's work"!! On the other side of the coin, there are some women out there that think they are divas; that everything should be about them. They believe that their man is there to wait on them hand and foot. Both of these situations scream disrespect to me!!

Who exactly do you think you are, treating another human being like this, especially one that you are supposed to be in love with?

Why can't we just treat each other equally? If we both essentially want the same things out of life, why can't we work together? When something needs to be done, just do it! Don't leave it for the other one to do when they get home.

Women are generally the multi-taskers. I'm not saying there aren't men that multi-task... remember I am speaking in general. The difference is women just do what needs to be done; they don't need or expect constant appreciation, verbally or otherwise. Men on the other hand, do need constant appreciation; essentially they need their egos stroked often.

No one follows the woman around thanking her for doing the dishes, laundry, paying the bills, cleaning the bathroom, etc. If someone was doing this, she would probably find it quite irritating. Most women truly have to make a conscious effort to always be thanking the man for his help. Women aren't very good at this, but we have to try.

Although women don't __need__ constant verbal appreciation, it does make them feel good to be thanked every now and then. It doesn't hurt anything to say, "I realize you work your ass off to make our life a good place to be and I truly do appreciate everything you do". This statement works both for men and women.

I realize I am not using "wife" and "husband" terms, but lets face it, this day and age there are just as many people not married, as married. That is one change that people seem to have made without much effort. I'm not saying that is a good thing, just making a point that people can change if they really want to.

My thought is, it is all about __respect.__ It doesn't matter whether you are the man or the woman. You need to treat each other as you would want to be treated. I think a lot of things would change and a lot of couples would get along better, if we would take a minute out of our precious time and give a little consideration to our partner in life. Before you do something, anything, just run it thru your brain; what would my partner think about this? What would I think or how would I feel, if the tables were turned?

We do have some differences, but let us accept the ones we can not change, and put a little effort into the rest of them.

What Exactly Are You Thinking? 16

Chapter 2

LET MEN BE MEN, WOMEN BE WOMEN

As human beings, we all have differences; but basically we all want the same thing out of life. <u>Respect from our partner.</u>

All of us need bonding time with our friends. Is it really a big deal if there is a "Girls' Night Out" or "Guys' Night Out" every so often?!! Maybe even a weekend getaway. I don't care who you are, or how much in love with your partner you are, you still need a little down time away from each other. I truly believe it will make your relationship better in the long run.

So he wants to go fishing with the guys one weekend, don't be a bitch about it; don't give him the "You never spend any time with me" bullshit. Just happily help him pack his stuff, tell him to have a good time and enjoy the time you now have to yourself.

The same thing goes for the women, if they need to go "Be Women" for a weekend, don't question why they want to go lay around a spa and relax, or whatever it is they choose to do. Just send them on their way with a smile on your face.

A mistake a lot of people make, is constantly calling the one trying to have a little down time! This definitely screams no trust. Just let them enjoy themselves and you enjoy the time you have to yourself at home. When they return, you will have lots to talk about. If you are calling every waking moment, when they return home, you already know all the details. Plus you are irritating the shit out of the one trying to relax!

It can be an amazing thing how different the attitude is when you return. A little time that is totally about you, not your partner, not your job, not your children, <u>JUST YOU</u>. This can transform you into a totally different person.

Men and women generally like to spend money on different things too. Again, don't try to understand why your partner likes to buy what he or she does. Just accept the fact that is what makes them happy. Let it be.

Now, having said all that, we all have to learn the difference between wants and needs. Obviously we can't buy every little thing we want and we damn sure can't be gone having down time constantly either. What I'm trying to get at, is, together we can find a happy medium.

As far as the finance end of things, you need to agree on a <u>realistic</u> budget. Budget money for both family fun and individual fun. Decide together what you want to do as family fun, and then let it be an individual decision on the individual fun.

One last thought:

I know there are a few men out there that think if they start helping around the house, that isn't manly!! This is total crap!! This day and age you will be considered more of a "Man", if you help your partner with all aspects of your life, not just the ones you prefer. Do you think she gets to do only what she wants to do? Hell no.

Again, treat your partner in the manner you would like to be treated!

Chapter 3

WHAT'S FOR DINNER?

As a general rule, this statement is not a good one, for anyone!!

You might say "What's for dinner, it sure smells good"; now this would probably earn you a few points. This is not usually how it goes! More likely, one of you, usually the woman, comes home, doesn't even get the door closed before her man says "What's for dinner?" Are you trying to start a fight? This is a pretty sure way to get it done!! What you are really saying is "It is beneath me to cook, but I sure expect you to do it!" She is thinking, are you kidding me? "Can I just have 20 minutes to relax? Most men like a little down time when they get off work, what would make you think a woman would be any different?

Next thought…. has it ever occurred to you men that the meals are another full-time job, which usually falls on the woman's shoulders? You have to constantly be thinking ahead of time, thawing things out, making sure you have the refrigerator and cupboards stocked, thinking about what sounds good. Has it ever entered your mind how happy your partner would be if she came thru the door to the smell of dinner cooking? Novel idea isn't it!!!!!

I feel safe in saying all women would love the opportunity to say "What's for dinner, it sure smells good!" Cooking really isn't that hard, pretty much if you can read, you can do it. I guarantee most women who came home to a meal being cooked, wouldn't care what it was. They would just think it was great that for once, they got to sit down and have a toddy, relax a bit while their partner was doing the cooking.

You will really earn points if you suck it up and clean the mess up too!! And this doesn't mean just what is in the sink. This means all the pots, pans, dishes, wiping down the counter tops and stove. After all, this is what she normally has to do every night, after she gets done putting dinner on the table!

How about trying this, the first one home starts dinner. As everyone else shows up, they jump right in and help, and this means until the work is done, not until you are done eating!! Then you can all sit down and relax together.

What Exactly Are You Thinking? 24

Chapter 4

SEX OR LACK OF

Supposedly it is a proven fact that men have more of a sex drive than women. That they think about it every hour on the hour during their day, while most women who are busy, doing several of their full-time jobs, running life in general, don't find sex being one of the top priority thoughts of their day.

I gotta tell ya, after a woman puts in a full day at work, goes to the grocery store, stops at the cleaners, etc, etc, etc. Then, comes home to her partner sitting in his chair, waiting for her to cook dinner, the last thing she is thinking is what position they might have sex in that night!! She is thinking I gotta get thru the next four hours of my day so I can finally fall into bed. Meanwhile you are relaxing happily in your chair, so when it comes time to go to the bedroom, you're all revved up ready to go!!

I guarantee you if she came home to you cooking or cleaning, mainly just anything to help her out to get the rest of her day over with, she would be a lot more likely to get in the romantic mood. There truly isn't anything sexier to a woman, than a man cooking or cleaning. I know, you men are thinking this is bullshit; you women are 100% with me! Why don't you men ask your significant other this question, you might be surprised at the response.

Now before your brain starts running wild with the idea that every time you want sex, you will just cook or clean, I am not saying this will happen each and every time you help out. But I will say, if you just make it a normal thing to help her, you will find she likes sex too. It's just more fun when you have a little energy to put into it, instead of just laying there taking it, for your mate's sake. Some call this "Taking One For The Team".

That statement might be a bit harsh for a few of you to admit, but I imagine most of you have experienced this situation at least once in your life. I've always wondered, does this situation really make a man feel manly?! I would think having the woman actually want you, would be a lot more fulfilling.

Again, the world is stuck on the idea that men have more of a sex drive than women, so the women should take care of this for them. How about instead of you men whining about this all the time, you actually try to do something about it!!

Why should this be any different than anything else in life, you have to put some effort into most things before you get a reward.

A small amount of effort sometimes will take you a long ways.

Chapter 5

PUT THE SHIT ON THE TABLE

Hopefully all of you realize by now, that men are not mind readers!! Women aren't either, but it seems to me it is usually the women that do the hinting around, they can't seem to just say what they need to say. Men do not like game playing or having to try to figure out what the female is trying to say, or why she is bawling her head off. If you have something to say, don't sugar coat it, just put the shit on the table in plain English and they will get it. Now I realize this is easier said than done for some of you, but maybe this is something you could work on.

Fortunately this is a trait that the females in my family are well-known for. I'm sure our husbands from time to time would appreciate a little sugar coating, but we just flat never learned how to do it! We were taught to be up front and that honesty is the best policy. We just put the shit on the table, it will either piss you off or not, but we will certainly get to the bottom of the issue, in a hurry!!

Too many people keep their feelings locked up inside, giving them a gut ache, because they don't want to hurt anyone's feelings. This is a nice thought, but usually doesn't work so well! All this does is to prolong the agony and your partner keeps running around wondering what the heck is wrong with you. I'm not saying to just fly off the handle every time something doesn't go your way, you can take a little time and think about it, as my husband says, "Say it to yourself, then if it sounds good, you can say it out loud".

For example, when you say to a man, "You need to be more into this relationship", you might as well be speaking a foreign language to him. He does not have a clue what you might be wanting from him. You need to be very blunt:

> *"I need more public affection..."*
> *"I want you to hold my hand..."*
> *"I want you to put your arm around me..."*
> *"I want you to give me a kiss on the cheek now and then...."*

I want you to discuss your important issues in life with me... This is supposed to be a partnership, don't act like your decisions don't have any effect on me.... Whatever it is that you need, put it in plain, black and white, blunt as you can make it, English. Believe me, he will appreciate this. It will make his life a lot easier. He wants to make you happy, but you have to hold up your end of the deal too. Always remember this statement, "Say What You Mean, and Mean What You Say". Don't say one thing and then turn around and do the opposite.

Unless, of course you are trying to make your situation a lot worse than it already is!! Believe it or not, some people do this, trying to make it so miserable for their partner, that the partner will finally get his/her fill of all the bullshit and decide to end the relationship. Pretty much they want out, but don't have the back bone to do anything about it. So they play this little game until the partner can't take it any more, makes the first move to end it, then everyone will blame your partner and you will be the one everyone feels sorry for!! This is sooooo chicken shit; this is the all-time low of disrespect. Again, don't play games; just put the shit on the table.

Chapter 6

THE TELEVISION

Believe it or not, these things are often trouble makers in a relationship. First of all men and women usually don't like the same kinds of shows. Every now and then you run across one that both of you are willing to watch, but for the most part, women like chick flicks, soap operas, Travel Channel, What Not To Wear, etc. and guys like shoot em' up bang bang movies, The History Channel, blood and gore or sports.

What really pisses me off, is when the guy can watch whatever he chooses, at whatever volume he chooses, which is usually blaring, and the woman is expected to either put up with it, or go to a different room. Now if the woman wants to watch a soap opera, for example, some men, for some reason, think they can throw a fit about this, because they think it is stupid!! Who gives a shit what they think?!! I am an adult; I can choose what I want to watch on TV! Do you want me telling you what to watch? I didn't think so.

Do you really think that women think football is any more intelligent than soap operas? (I realize there are some women in the world that love sports) Are a bunch of grown men chasing a little ball around, tackling each other any more or less stupid than a soap opera? Personally, there is nothing in the world I have less interest in than football. Hey, to each their own.

Everybody has their stuff they like to watch on TV, so take turns, find something you both like, or better yet, turn the damn thing off and go play cards. Do something together.

Chapter 7

HORMONES

As far as I know, hormones are a proven issue with people, contrary to some people's beliefs; it is not all in the woman's head. It is also a proven fact that men, yes the male species also have hormones!!!!

Everyone is a little different as far as when the hormonal imbalance thing starts happening, but it does happen in all of us, and it starts at a much younger age than you might think.

Instead of trying to ignore this situation, just meet it head on. Get yourself to a bio-identical doctor, take the tests, and get on the hormones you need. Start making progress towards feeling better. I guarantee you will both be a lot happier when the hot flashes, low energy level, moodiness, etc. stop. Both sets of attitudes will be a lot better when you get your hormones in balance.

Some people think they can't afford hormones, I think you can't afford <u>not to have</u> hormones. You need to give some serious thought to what is important in life. Most people seem to find money for their bad habits in life, drinking, smoking, chewing, etc. I personally think your health should be in the #1 slot. I totally believe, where there is a will, there is a way. Just set your mind to it, it is all worth it when you feel young again.

You only have one body and you only get to go thru life once, so let's make the best of it.

For you people who are embarrassed by all this….…..Do you really think the world still thinks you are in your thirties? You aren't fooling anyone, just making life more miserable for everyone involved. I will guarantee one thing, if you think ignoring this issue will make it go away, you are sadly mistaken.

These are the options I see:

a) You can admit to yourself you are getting older, deal with it, and feel great. Be glad you are alive to deal with it.

or

b) You can continue to wake up in a pool of water, having hot flashes at the worst possible moments, but still trying to act like this isn't happening to you…….. total embarrassment.

As far as you men go, when you finally get shit full of dragging your ass around because you just don't have the energy you used to have, then maybe you will start reading up a little on testosterone, you know the all mighty hormone you are so proud to be full of!!

You could even wait longer, until the day comes when you still want sex, but can't get it up any more. Then maybe you will start believing the hormone thing isn't just for women!!

Why would anyone think that only women's bodies change as they age?

Chapter 8

MARRIAGE COUNSELING

When you have arrived at this point in life, it is damn sure time to get off your high horse and start admitting what is truly going on in your life. To a lot of people this is an embarrassing moment, they want to keep it a secret; they want the world to think they have the perfect marriage……. no problems here!!!

The way I look at it is, if one or both of you have a problem, the problem should concern both of you; it damn sure is going to affect both of you. One way or another, it has to be dealt with.

Now, I will admit it really isn't anyone else's business, but word always gets out. Part of the problem is that women need to talk about their problems, in detail. They don't necessarily want a solution, they just need to vent. This is not an easy thing for a man to understand, his natural response is to solve the problem. This is the last thing the woman wants you to do! In all reality, as hard as it is, if the man can just sit there quietly and let her vent, not offering a solution, not saying a word, she will feel better and you will eventually see your great effort was worth it. Women just have to vent, then they can start wrapping their head around a solution.

If the man can't quietly listen or just doesn't want to listen to all the gory details, over and over again, he has to accept the fact that she is going to discuss their personal situation with someone else. She has to vent!

Usually what I see happening is the man doesn't want to listen, or can't stand to listen to all of it, so the woman talks to someone, sister, friend, or stranger, then the guy is all pissed off, at both his wife, and the listener. Actually he ought to be happy she has someone to talk to, and if they are a decent person, they won't share this with the general public. What is she supposed to do, let all this build up inside, until the top of her head blows off? Or you come home one day and she greets you at the door with fire shooting out of her eyes and you get the ass-chewin' of a lifetime.

For a woman, she has to vent, so if you really want to be the sounding board, then step right up, but if you don't, don't get your nose all out of joint when she goes to someone else, just keep your mouth shut about it. You deal with it your way; let her deal with it her way.

The important thing here is that both of you care enough about your marriage to admit that you need help and actually try to do something about it, versus taking the easy way out, DIVORCE. You ought to be proud of the fact you are doing all you can to save your marriage. Quit wasting valuable energy on shit that doesn't really matter. Don't sweat the small stuff, gossip is small stuff. Who really gives a shit who says what to whom? To begin with, probably half of what is said is total bullshit, by the time it goes thru three or four different mouths. Sometimes no one repeated anything, someone just wanted to start a little gossip, so they did!! When you get all pissy about it and start letting it ruin your day, they have won. You have wasted all your energy on bullshit that doesn't matter, instead of concentrating on the #1 issue, you and your spouse.

If you are spending the time and money to see a counselor, don't you think you owe it to each other to make the most of this time. Spend 100% of this time working as hard as you can on your problems.

The hardest part of this is you have got to be totally honest, or all of this is for naught. You have to have enough back bone to take it when the therapist hands your ass to you. This can be a very humbling experience, but you have got to get to the root of the problem, before you can start fixing it. Don't be thinking all the problems are your partner's; that is never the case.

The other thing that happens is you are listening to your partner bald face lie to the therapist, or purposely leave part of the story out. Do not let this happen, do not get all pissed off, just open your mouth and finish the necessary details. The therapist can't fix the problem if he/she only has part of the information. This gets you no where fast!! Total waste of time and money.

No one ever said it would be easy talking to a counselor. You both will probably discover things about yourself that you don't particularly care for. However hard it is, just keep moving forward and keep your common goal in mind, your marriage.

Chapter 9

OVER THE YEARS, THINGS CHANGE

It seems to me I see this happening a lot. The couple has been married for 25+ years. In the beginning he was the sole bread winner, she was the stay at home mom who cooked, cleaned, had babies, did laundry, etc. She had plenty on her plate, but she did it all, because that was her "Full-time job", her part of this relationship. Then when the man got home, his day ended. At this point she added to her list of "To-do's", to wait on him. Not that this was ever fair, but back in the day, that is the way it was.

Now, the kids are grown, married, having grandkids, whatever, but it is now just the two of you. She now has a full-time job, but for some reason the husband thinks every thing should stay the same as before. She should be able to work full-time, keep up with the household duties, and continue to wait on his ass hand and foot.

What is wrong with this picture? Is there any part of this that makes you think the husband has any respect for his wife? How about appreciating the fact that she has been Wonder Woman for the last 25 years, instead of expecting it for another 25!!!!! Doesn't she deserve a little reprieve?

Now, I have heard this statement more than once, "I didn't make her go get a job, if that is what she chooses to do, she has to figure out how to get everything in life done. I'm fine with her staying home, not having a full-time job. I still want to be waited on, I like it when she does all the household stuff. Talk about a self-centered bullshit attitude!!! You wonder why people end up divorced after 25 years of being married? Everyone thinks, why would you get a divorce after being married so long? If you've made it this far, surely you can make it the rest of the way.

Most instances, the wife isn't saying she regrets the past 25 years, but life changes, she has put her time in at home, she has helped raise the kids, now she wants to be a little more independent, spread her wings a little, and do something different.
Why shouldn't she be able to do this? And without you making her totally miserable?

Do you really think it will kill you to help around your house a little bit, after all, she has been doing it all for you for years. Isn't the important thing to live happily ever after? Or

*are you just concerned with you
living happily ever after?*

*When she finally gets shit full of it,
leaves your ass to go run and play
with her girlfriends, don't call me
looking for sympathy!*

Chapter 10

Cutting The Umbilical Cord

Have you ever heard a man called a "Mama's Boy" or a woman called "Daddy's Little Girl"? These are not compliments!!!!!!

Showing love and respect to your parents is one thing, but when you get married, you need to cut the umbilical cord. Pretty much if you are still talking to a parent each and every day, you probably haven't got this done yet.

When you grow up and start a life of your own, you need to act like an adult, deal with and discuss your problems in life with each other; don't drag the parents into it. When one of you starts talking to a parent about personal problems, it puts the parents in a hot spot. You don't want to tarnish their opinion of your spouse, but it is very easy to do, if you start discussing too much with them. Even if the situation gets better, it is hard for them to forget what was said. I guarantee you don't know every detail about their personal life, nor should you.

Parents can pretty much make or break their children. They are so happy taking care of their children, they don't even think about what a mess they could be creating for their future daughter or son-in-laws.

If you don't teach them normal, every day life things, like laundry, cooking, cleaning, etc., they go into adult life thinking someone else is surely going to keep doing all this stuff for them.

It's much easier on them to just teach them how to be self-sufficient from the get-go. A lot of mothers, I think, just assume their little boys will marry someone who is willing to do all this stuff for them. And they might, but odds are in this day and age, it very well could be an independent woman, now they've got problems!!

Same with spoiled "Daddy's Girls"; who wants to start their adult life with a spoiled brat that assumes you will do everything for her? Or every time you don't, she calls Daddy.

I'm not saying to never talk to your parents, but you need to consider what they need to hear and what is really none of their concern. They raised you to age 18, don't you think they've done their job? How about showing them that they did do a good job raising you? Show them you are quite capable of acting like an adult, dealing with your own problems without dragging them into all of it.

Chapter 11

I'm Your Wife, Not Your Mother

Most women get married because they want a partner in life; someone to share life with, do things with, accomplish goals with, not someone to mother.

Too many men get married thinking the wife wants to cook three meals a day, do the laundry, clean the house, etc. (Everything Mom did for them) I will admit, there are a few women out there that live for this, if you want one and can find one, more power to you. For the rest of the world, act like an adult, take on the extra responsibility. Act like an equal partner, make your spouse proud to tell the world how you both work together to make life good.

Look around and see what needs done, anything from mowing the lawn to doing the laundry. If it needs done, just do it, don't wait for your spouse to it. If it is something you really don't enjoy doing, your spouse might not enjoy it either, but the bottom line is, it has to be done.

If you have the deal that one of you does the inside work, the other the outside work, whatever the agreement, hold your end of the deal up. Don't make your partner be the bad guy because you aren't holding up your end of the deal. I hear this all the time, "My wife is such a nag, if she would just get off my ass, I would get these things done." If you would just get your share done in the first place, she wouldn't have to bitch at you. Believe me she doesn't want to have to act like your mother, any more than you want her too! Do you find yourself having to get on her about keeping her share done?

(I doubt it) If you are screwing around, procrastinating and your partner gets bitchy, you only have yourself to blame for this.

I realize the general consensus is that men don't pay attention to, or care about details like women do.....I think this is a total cop out. This is what the world has allowed to become a general statement, so everyone seems to fall into it, instead of putting a little effort into paying attention. You can't tell me that if the sink is full of dirty dishes, a man doesn't notice this as he adds another dish to the pile!! He doesn't notice this because he doesn't want to do the dishes. He knows his wife will eventually get tired of the mess and do something about it. Yes, she usually does, but I can guarantee this does not impress her in the least. And every time this happens, she is making a mental note of it. How about doing a few things that will make her happy, make her feel proud of you, show her a little respect.

Make a general list of "Things That Need To Be Done". Lay it on the desk so both of you can work on it. If you are the pusher partner, the one that constantly has to push the other to help, the one that is considered bitchy, this gets old, fast. If you both make an effort to get at least one thing done per day, before or after work, it is no great effort on either of you. Now, things are getting done, your place looks nice and you've got something to be proud of.

I think it's a great feeling when people comment about how nice your place looks, and the greatest feeling is to know both of you have done it. To know that your partner in life really is your partner in life.

It helps a lot if you both have the same goals, but even if you don't, meet in the middle. You have got to work at keeping the other one happy or pretty soon the pusher partner gets tired of pushing and then you've got major problems.

What Exactly Are You Thinking?   60

CLOSING STATEMENT –

I just don't think this has to be as difficult as it is. Just live by the following ten rules:

#1 Treat your partner in life like you want to be treated, show a little respect.

#2 Treat your partner in life like you want to be treated, show a little respect.

#3 Treat your partner in life like you want to be treated, show a little respect.

#4 Treat your partner in life like you want to be treated, show a little respect.

#5 Treat your partner in life like you want to be treated, show a little respect.

#6 Treat your partner in life like you want to be treated, show a little respect.

#7 Treat your partner in life like you want to be treated, show a little respect.

#8 Treat your partner in life like you want to be treated, show a little respect.

#9 Treat your partner in life like you want to be treated, show a little respect.

#10 Treat your partner in life like you want to be treated, show a little respect.

I hope some of you have found this book helpful, and will try to make your relationship with your partner a happier place to be for both of you.

www.ingramcontent.com/pod-product-compliance
Lightning Source LLC
Chambersburg PA
CBHW060221290526
45789CB00003B/1357